The

Connell Short Guide

to

J.B. Priestley's

An Inspector Calls

by

David Hughes

Contents

Introduction

A girl's face haunts the play, a girl alone and dying. She wants to die. Pregnant and penniless, she has swallowed disinfectant. This is Eva Smith, the central figure, a heroine who doesn't even appear in her own play. Forgotten by the wealthy elite who have abused her, she was once "a lively good-looking girl". Her story has been lost. It is the task of the Inspector to reclaim it.

An Inspector Calls is set in 1912, when a mysterious police inspector visits the wealthy Birling family, and exposes how each of them has contributed to the death of this impoverished young woman, Eva Smith. Priestley wrote the play in 1944, at a time when Britain was about to decide its direction after World War II; he wrote it to make the case for socialism and to evoke the inequalities and, as Priestley saw it, injustice of society in 1912, while also seeking to remind his audience that not nearly enough had changed since the days before World War One.

On one level, *An Inspector Calls* is a detective story, a whodunit where suspects are questioned in turn, and where each is found guilty. It is, perhaps, a ghost story, too. It is a family drama, where secrets and tensions emerge to disrupt the seeming harmony of an engagement party. But much more importantly it is a social commentary, where the arrogance and indifference of the ruling class are brought to book by a mysterious figure who argues "we are responsible for each other", and a morality play, where characters embody vices, and are brought to judgement.

So how successful is it, as a play, and how relevant is it to the world we live in today?

Let us first look at the way the story unfolds.

What happens in *An Inspector Calls?*

Act One

It is 1912, and our play is set in Brumley, a fictional north Midlands town. The curtain rises. We see a dining room, and a family around the table. These are the Birlings, relaxing after dinner with a guest, as Edna, the parlour maid, clears away their "champagne glasses" and "dessert plates". The "good solid furniture" tells of prosperity, and the "evening dress" worn by the characters assures us these are respectable people.

Mr Birling, a self-made man in his "middle fifties", sits at the head of the table, while his wife sits at the far end. In between them, upstage and facing the audience, sits their daughter Sheila, "a pretty girl in her early twenties", and her fiancé Gerald Croft, an "attractive chap about thirty". Facing these two, downstage, and with his back to the audience, is Eric, the Birlings' son, also in his "early twenties".

The dinner is to celebrate the engagement of Sheila to Gerald, the son of a wealthy industrialist. The atmosphere is cheerful and complacent. Birling uses the occasion to express his confidence that neither worker unrest nor talk of war with Germany will pose a threat to their way of life. Birling identifies himself with "progress", mentioning the new "unsinkable" *Titanic* as evidence that history is on the side of capitalists like himself, those who believe society is based on the idea that "a man has to mind his own business and look after himself".

All seems well. And yet there are questions. Why did Gerald keep away from Sheila last summer? Why is Eric drinking? Why is he provoking his father, or checking himself when he was about to speak of some woman he remembers? There is more to all this than meets the eye, and a "sharp ring of a front door bell" interrupts Mr Birling in full flow, just as he is dismissing socialist ideas of "community and all that nonsense". Edna announces the arrival of an "Inspector Goole".

The Inspector is an impressive figure, with a direct manner. He brings news of a young woman, Eva Smith, who has committed suicide by drinking disinfectant. Birling is confident this has nothing to do with him, but the Inspector produces a photograph of the girl. Birling remembers her. This was autumn 1910. She was a worker in his factory, and her troubles began when he dismissed her for demanding higher wages. Birling denies any responsibility for her death – this happened eighteen months ago – but the Inspector believes this is part of a "chain of events" which led from Eva losing her job, to her suicide.

Quickly, others begin to be involved. Gerald is shocked when he hears Eva also went by the name of Daisy Renton. Sheila is distressed when she learns Eva was dismissed from her next job at Milwards, a local department store. It was December 1910. A customer had complained. Sheila realises it was her. She had been trying on a new dress, against the advice of her mother and an assistant. Eva held the dress against herself to make a point. It suited her better than Sheila. As Sheila tried it on in the mirror, she caught Eva "smiling" at her fellow assistant as if to say "Doesn't she look awful?" Sheila had Eva sacked. Unlike her father, Sheila understands now she was wrong. She feels it is "a rotten shame". She feels responsible. She also sees Gerald is hiding something. The Inspector "knows". Act One ends dramatically. Gerald and Sheila are confronted by the Inspector, who "looks steadily and searchingly at them. The curtain falls.

Act Two

Sheila and Gerald argue. Sheila sees Gerald is being "evasive". She insists on hearing what Gerald has to say to the Inspector. Gerald says she is staying out of spite, "to see somebody else put through it". Sheila is angry. He doesn't know her. He is mistaking her for "a selfish, vindictive creature". Sheila is growing in independence and understanding. She sees Mrs Birling and Eric will also be involved. She sees it is no good Mrs Birling adopting a gracious, patronising manner towards the Inspector. She warns her mother she "mustn't try to build up a kind of wall between us and that girl". Now Gerald tells his story.

By January 1911, Eva had changed her name to Daisy Renton. Gerald "happened" to meet her at the bar in The Palace music hall in Brumley. This is a "favourite haunt of women of the town" (prostitutes). He noticed Daisy, who was "very pretty", and "young and fresh and charming". Daisy was being harassed by a "notorious womaniser", Alderman Meggarty, and gave Gerald "a glance that was nothing less than a cry for help". Gerald began to help Daisy. He offered her a meal and arranged for her to live in "a nice little set of rooms" at "Morgan Terrace", which he was looking after for a friend. Gerald emphasises that he "didn't install her there so I could make love to her", but he admits that she became his "mistress", and says "I suppose it was inevitable".

By the first week of September 1911, however, the relationship was "coming to an end". Gerald "broke it off" before going on a business trip. Daisy expected this, and "hadn't expected it to last". He insisted on giving her money, which she reluctantly accepted. Daisy then left for two months at a "seaside town". Here she wrote a diary which showed her disappointment at the end of the relationship, that "there'd never be anything as good again for her."

As she listens to Gerald's story, Sheila responds. She now understands where he was last summer. Her anger is vented in sarcastic comments about him being a "hero" and a "Fairy Prince". She wants to know if he was in love with Daisy, as she tries to gauge the depth of his betrayal. As Gerald leaves, upset by memories of Daisy, Sheila hands back the engagement ring. She is relieved at least that he has been "honest". She respects him more than she did. On his part, Gerald asks her permission to return later. Here, mid-way through the play, the impact of the Inspector is felt in the separation of Sheila and Gerald. Now attention turns to Mrs Birling.

Mrs Birling is reluctant to tell her story. It appears she had met Eva at the Brumley Women's Charity Organisation, where she decided who should receive gifts of charity. This was only two weeks ago, in the spring of 1912. Eva needed help. She was unmarried, pregnant, and tried to pass herself of as a "Mrs Birling". This provokes the real Mrs Birling. She refuses to help. Eva was guilty of "impertinence", "disgusting" sexual impropriety, and "telling us a pack of lies". Eva didn't want to say who the father was. Mrs Birling feels "a girl of that sort" was also not entitled to moral scruples. Morality was her business. Eva was not “a deserving case”. The father should be made to pay. As usual, Sheila is the first to see what is happening. The more Mrs Birling blames the father, the more she is condemning her own son. Eric is the father. Eric enters dramatically as Act Two ends. He is next.

Act Three

In November 1911, Eva Smith was again at the Palace music hall. Eric had a vague idea “some woman... wanted her to go there”. Eva was now in peril of prostitution. Eric was “squiffy”, “in that state when a chap easily turns nasty”. He forced himself into her rooms in a threatening way, and “that’s when it happened”. He had sex with her. He effectively raped her (though the text isn’t explicit here). They met again by chance, made love, and eventually she became pregnant. Eric was “in a hell of a state about it”, and offered Eva money. He even offered to marry her, but she wouldn’t, dismissing him as if he were a “kid”. All that was left for Eva was the Brumley Women’s Charity Organisation.

Eric’s story causes more family upset. Mrs Birling is shocked to hear Eric drinks. She even has to leave the room when she learns of his sexual encounter with Eva. Mr Birling is apoplectic when he discovers that Eric stole money from the works to keep a pregnant Eva going. Eric’s buried anger against his parents is emerging. His father has been domineering, a bully. Eric now turns on him.

He says "you're not the kind of father a chap could go to when he's in trouble". He accuses his mother of killing Eva and the baby who would have been her first grandchild, saying "you killed them both".

The Inspector interrupts the family arguments. He is about to leave. He ends with the lesson of the play, its most important statement. This is that we live in a society, that "We don't live alone. We are members of one body. We are responsible for one another". He leaves with the warning that "if men will not learn that lesson, then they will be taught it in fire and blood and anguish."

After the Inspector leaves, there is a family scene. This balances the one before he came, though it is very different in mood. Sheila asks if he were a real inspector, and Gerald returns with news from a local constable that there is no Inspector Goole. Gerald develops the idea that the investigation was an elaborate "hoax". He points out how the Inspector could have been talking about different girls, since he only showed the photograph(s) to one person at a time. Birling telephones Colonel Roberts who confirms there is no inspector. Gerald drives things further forward by phoning the infirmary to see if a girl has died that evening. No – no one has committed suicide for months.

Without the Inspector, the characters are free to react how they like. Mr and Mrs Birling are eager to discredit the Inspector, and present him as "a fake", a "socialist or some kind of crank", and

An Inspector Calls starring Eileen Moore, Olga Lindo, Brian Worth, and Alastair Sim

Gerald contributes to this process with his questions. Mr Birling is delighted at the prospect of avoiding public shame, and attaining his knighthood. Sheila and Eric, however, form an alliance, and feels "it's what happened to the girl and what we all did to her that matters". The older generation and Gerald seek to erase the past, and deny any "responsibility" for what they did. Sheila and Eric face up to it. Sheila has grown. Eric has expressed his buried resentments, and accepted he was wrong.

When it appears no girl has died, Gerald renews his proposal to Sheila, saying "What about this ring?" The play ends, however, with another kind of "ring". The "telephone rings sharply". It is dramatic news. A girl has died swallowing disinfectant, and a police inspector is on his way. In a final coup de theatre, Priestley shows the Birlings are unable to escape their "responsibility" for Eva's death. They will pay for their actions. Justice will be done, and the ending is also effective by pointing to the Inspector's lesson that we must learn from our errors, or suffer as we repeat them, "in blood and fire and anguish".

Why is social class so important in *An Inspector Calls?*

Look again at the opening scene, the sheer materialism, the consumption: the splendid "evening dress", the cigars, the fine port, the "first-class" dinner. Gerald is giving Sheila a ring. Sheila has been buying clothes for Gerald's benefit. The dining room has "good solid furniture of the period". Edna the servant is catering to their every need.

The Birlings are successful, socially ambitious. Wealth appears in their clothes, furniture, food, and drink, the valuable objects they offer one another. They are confirming their social status. Birling tells Gerald this engagement to Sheila "means a tremendous lot to me", as it will pave the way to Gerald's family company working with Birling and Company "for lower costs and higher prices". Birling hints to Gerald that he is expecting a knighthood. Mrs Birling is in control of conduct at the table, reminding Birling it is not good manners to compliment the cook when dining in company, and correcting the behaviour of the children. She understands that good manners make wealth seem natural, proper, and well deserved. Manners are an index of the rank to which they aspire.

The Birlings have acquired wealth. They want to preserve it. This process is supported by the ideas they have, what Marx calls "ideology", a set of social beliefs which present their wealth as justifiable, while also concealing its real sources. Ideology is a kind of "cover story", and Birling's after dinner speech expresses his beliefs. Birling speaks as "a hard-headed business man". He defends "the interests of Capital". He justifies the interests of the ruling class who own the factories and means of production, and set the wages. For him and his class, it is a time of "peace and prosperity and rapid progress everywhere", and those who agitate for the rights of the working class or "Labour" are fighting the tide of history. To think otherwise is "nonsense".

The Birlings and Gerald all present their treatment of Eva as justifiable. Each of them sees her through the prism of this ideology, the social values and attitudes of their class. Unconsciously, they believe this: they are in the right; Eva is working class; she is to be disposed of like an object. For Birling, she is a number in a business equation. She is twenty two shillings and sixpence a week, not twenty five shillings. It is morally necessary to protect his capital, to dispense with her. It was his "duty to keep labour costs down... she had to go". As the customer at Milwards, Sheila is always right, and "that girl" had been "impertinent" to one of her betters. She had transgressed the rules of polite behaviour which ensures those lower down defer to those higher up. For Sheila, deference to the elite matters more than someone's livelihood. Mrs Birling can also provide an ideological story or two. The poor can be divided into the "deserving" poor, and undeserving cases like Eva. This means Eva's poverty is her own fault, the result of her "disgusting" sexual offences, what she deserves. The Birlings are in the right. Eva is to be disposed of, however extreme her plight has become.

As for the young men, there are double standards of sexual morality readily available to justify their behaviour. In visiting the Palace music hall, the "favourite haunt of women of the town" Gerald is simply being an "easy, well-bred young man about town", behaving as rich young men do. Eva may hope for love, but she comes to see their relationship is doomed by beliefs about class. It cannot be. It is "inevitable" that an "affair" between a poor girl and the son of Lord Croft will come to nothing. Gerald may be "distressed" when he realises Eva is dead, but it doesn't last. He is soon back offering Sheila her engagement ring. No matter he has betrayed her, and Eva. A dynastic marriage between Birlings and Crofts makes perfect social sense. Even Gerald fails to see Eva as an autonomous and independent young woman.

Eric is even worse. He is so drunk he doesn't even try to justify what he does. He says "I couldn't remember her name or where she lived. It was very vague." Eric, like all of them, does what he wants with her. She doesn't have a "name", an identity. He just takes her. When he finds out she was pregnant, he responds "I was in a hell of a state about it", and he gives her money he has stolen from the works, money which was part of the profit made from the labour of workers like Eva.

Viewed together, these attitudes have a single purpose and a single effect. They allow the wealthy characters to justify what they are doing. It was perfectly understandable how they behaved. It was "duty", "deference", "morality", or "marital suitability" which guided them. Their behaviour was reasonable. It was justified to treat Eva so.

Only Eric lacks a cover story for what he does.

In a way, though, Eric is the most honest of all of them in his treatment of Eva, and he clearly shows what is really going on. In what is perhaps the most disturbing line in the play, Eric says "I was in that state when a chap easily turns nasty –

and I threatened to make a row". Here Priestley takes the Woosterish notion of a "chap", and makes a connection with violence.

It may surprise us that a "chap" can be "nasty", but Eric is right. Each of the Birlings turns "nasty". They construct their moral positions, and find ways of justifying themselves. But in each case Eva is behaving in ways which challenge their sense of what is due someone in their position. And so they *punish* her. Birling talks of "capital", but there is real hostility in the way he decides to "come down sharply" on her. Sheila is "absolutely furious". Mrs Birling sets about Eva in a way Sheila describes correctly as "cruel and vile", and which Eric describes as murderous, "you killed her – and the child she'd have had too". There is a lot of anger directed towards Eva. And in each case it is because Eva has stepped out of line. The Birlings enjoy their position in the hierarchy. They have to protect it.

So the play exposes a social violence beneath the stories they tell. Each of them is finding ways of laundering class cruelty. What an example Mrs Birling is here, doing her good works at the Brumley Women's Charitable organisation. She talks of charity, love of one's neighbour. But she is really enjoying the chance to use her social position to decide the fate of others. She likes the gratifying sense of her own superiority, particularly if it can appear as morality.

It is no surprise, perhaps, that Eva herself

begins to internalise all this abuse, and social violence. She was a feisty class warrior at the strike at Birlings. She was a mischievous attendant at Milwards, a girl of spirit, wishing to rise in the world. But gradually she becomes demoralised, reduced to an object of men's attention because of her "soft brown hair and big dark eyes", a mistress for Gerald, a visitor at the Palace music hall, an unmarried mother and a charity case. And, in the end, of course, she *literally* internalises the violence meted out to her in the play. She takes her life by drinking disinfectant, "destroying herself" at the infirmary.

As we shall see, Eva's suicide is a complex act. She is completing the violence done to her. She is also reclaiming control of the body which had become a kind of commodity. Dying by "disinfectant" is also significant. It is a way of purifying herself of the contaminating effects of the Birlings. To understand more about this, we need to pay attention to her story. There is a lot in it. This is where the play gets really interesting.

What is the significance of Eva Smith?

Each of the dinner guests had power over Eva, and each abused that power. Each saw Eva in a way which was distorted according to particular social attitudes. The Inspector exposes this abuse, collects these episodes into a coherent account, and offers them the opportunity to accept their "responsibility".

But that's not the whole story.

What really happens to Eva?

She begins as a "lively good-looking girl", who is about to be promoted by Birling. She has the confidence to challenge the status quo, and demand "higher wages". She has "a lot to say – too much" about the rights of labour, so "she had to go". Two months of hardship follow before Milwards, but her confidence seems intact from the way she models the dress for Sheila, and the cheeky smile directed towards Miss Francis.

Eva Smith now becomes Daisy Renton. Using an alias suggests a shift in Eva, a loss of who she has been, and a wish to hide who she might be about to become. The new name of "Daisy" retains her youthful appeal and country origins, while "Renton" conveys a new sense of herself as a commodity, something for sale. She had been "Eva", with all its suggestion of a lost innocence and paradise, and she had been "Smith", with all its echoes of an agricultural economy founded upon craft, before industrialisation. Now she is struggling with the new realities of her life, which are leading her to the Palace music hall, and towards prostitution.

She is "young and fresh and charming and altogether out of place down there" in the Palace music hall – but she is there, nonetheless, "wedged... into a corner" by Alderman Meggarty "with that obscene fat carcass of his". Daisy is now the damsel in distress, trapped by the monster, awaiting rescue by her "wonderful Fairy Prince" (as Sheila calls Gerald). The fairy story elements of the scene hint at a deeper wish fulfilment in Eva as a young woman, another element to her femininity, a wish for love and romance.

With Gerald, moreover, Eva can also fulfill other fantasies entailed within femininity (as constructed at the time). The life at Morgan Terrace speaks to a wish for security, shared domesticity, and a fulfilling sexual relationship. Eva is in love with Gerald, and one feels she gives herself sexually to him, not in payment, but in the hope of a flourishing intimacy and eventual marriage. And yet, she is not able to be Eva. She is Daisy Renton. She is not the independent girl she was. She is dependent upon Gerald. She is in an intimate relationship, rehearsing married life, giving herself to a man, while not even using her own name. While she wants to feel she has been rescued, she also recognises she is imprisoned. As Gerald says "She told me she'd been happier than she'd ever been before – but that she knew it couldn't last – hadn't expected it to last. She didn't blame me at all. I wish to God she had now. Perhaps I'd feel better about it".

This is the decisive event in Eva's life. How *nobly* she behaves. No anger. No recrimination.

She lets him go, and goes away to "be quiet and remember". The relationship is now becoming a memory. She thinks about it "just to make it last longer". Depths are opening up in Eva's inner world. She is at the seaside, but it is autumn, and the weather is changing. She is introspective. She is writing a journal to express the stormy feelings which threaten her, and to hold onto memories of events which have gone for ever. She has given away her innocence. She is "fallen". She is Eve. She is Daisy Renton. She is mourning her loss. She is questioning herself. Who is to blame? Not Gerald. She loves Gerald. She is to blame. She is the one who fell.

Eva is exhibiting signs of what Freud calls "melancholia", a state similar to mourning. A loss of interest in the world, a loss of self-esteem, a carelessness about eating, and a "fixation" on a past love object – all these are evident in Eva. So, too, is the way that there is a conflict within her between the feelings she retains for Gerald, and the need to find someone else to blame for his disinterest. These are all elements of this pathology of loss and self-negation – and the similarity continues to the end. Freud also describes where "melancholia" leads. It leads to suicide.

Indeed, Eva's return to Brumley takes on added pathos. She is next seen in the Palace music hall. This is deeply contradictory. It may be she has lost her self-esteem, and is embarking upon prostitution – or it may be she has returned because she wants that moment again when she first saw Gerald. Both possibilities fit with our view of Eva as "fixated", as returning compulsively to past events, remembering them in a way which combines a loss of self-esteem with a love for Gerald. She could have gone anywhere. She went back to the bar at the music hall. She wants it to happen again. She knows it can't.

What does happen next is Eric. This is not "the Fairy Prince" who offers her lodgings, and who makes a point of asking for nothing in return. This is effectively a rapist who invades her lodgings, and probably her body, and who takes what he wants. For whatever reason, Eva does not press charges, and even allows a sexual relationship to develop – and one which lacks the feelings which were the point for her of her intimacy with Gerald. Nevertheless, the earlier Eva is still intact somewhere here. She will not take money which is stolen. She will not marry Eric when he does not love her.

Pregnant, unmarried, on the verge of motherhood, Eva continues to present a fluctuating femininity. In the play, she has bordered on being many kinds of woman: the country maid, the harlot, the mistress, the domestic angel, the fallen woman, and now the mother to be (without exactly being *any* of them). Eva is the central character. She dominates the action – but she doesn't appear in it. Eva is both present and absent, a puzzling elusive non-entity. If we try to codify her according to female types here, we see that *none* of them quite fits.

An Inspector Calls is presenting a critique of patriarchy alongside its exposure of the evils of social class. In 1912, indeed, Eva might have hoped to meet a woman who sympathised with sisterhood and female suffrage at the Brumley Women's Charitable Organisation, but she doesn't. She meets Mrs Birling, a woman who blames Eva for her plight first, and the young man second, a woman who is scornful towards Eva's story, and who does not believe a word she hears from "a girl of that sort". Mrs Birling is always unsettled by sexual impropriety, and she responds with aggression. At this point she finishes the job started by the young men in the story. As far as Mrs Birling is concerned, when it comes to Eva, the victim is to blame.

And so Eva dies. She swallows disinfectant, internalising the violence directed towards her, while seeking simultaneously to purify her body of the taints inflicted upon it. She lies upon the slab at the infirmary, her suicide a negation of herself which is simultaneously a refusal to direct any blame towards Gerald, the one person she loved in the story.

But this is not the end of her story.

For one thing, she is not actually dead for most of the play – she is about to die, if we remember that she has not yet reached the infirmary when

Gerald rings late in Act Three. For another, she is very much present in the play, a kind of ghost constantly being summoned by the Inspector to haunt the guilty. And, lastly, there may be something still missing from this account of her life: anger and a demand for vengeance which has been repressed. Freud tells us that suicide is *a desire for revenge*, that "no neurotic harbors thoughts of suicide which are not murderous impulses against others redirected upon [her] self". Eva still wants revenge. This is where the Inspector comes in. He is her alter ego. He is her fury at the whole pack of them. In her absence, he speaks the anger she could not say or acknowledge.

What should we make of the Inspector?

The Inspector's arrival is announced by "the sharp ring of a front door bell". He immediately has presence enough for two, "an impression of massiveness, solidity and purposefulness", as well as a judicial air, "a disconcerting habit of looking hard at the person he addresses". This determined figure will not be deflected by offers of port, social niceties, or hints about Birling's social influence. He speaks plainly about the "nasty mess" of Eva's death, is always "cutting through" irrelevancies, and methodically reconstructs the "chain of events" leading to Eva's death by following "one line of inquiry at a time".

The Inspector has purpose: to draw our attention back to Eva herself, her humanity, her autonomy, her rights, her independent life, her picture, her letters, her diary, and her dying body. The Birlings see her as a disruptive force, or a "very pretty girl" who behaves impertinently. The Inspector makes them face the consequences of their self-interest. Again and again, he returns to the imagery of Eva dying "after several hours of agony, tonight in the Infirmary". The Inspector brings them face to dying face with Eva here, as in the moments when he shows them her photograph. Through these motifs, and even more in the stories each is required to tell, the Inspector is insisting that they *see* Eva at last, and no longer hide behind convenient explanations which suit themselves and their class. They have to look him in the eyes. They have to look Eva in the eyes.

Who is the Inspector? Like Eva, his character has many sides. He begins as a detective in a murder mystery, addressing the guests in the drawing room, piecing together the hidden story. But this is no ordinary police investigation, and the Birlings rightfully question it. Sheila asks "but was he really a police inspector?", and Gerald discovers "That man wasn't a police inspector". Is he a "hoax", or a "fake", as Birling calls him? Perhaps he is "a Socialist or some sort of crank"?

No, because the ending removes that possibility – a girl *has* died, and "a police inspector is on his way". Will this be the same Inspector? How odd that would be...

And if he investigated Eva's death *before* it happened, he must be some kind of premonition, a supernatural figure? The clue is in the name: Inspectre Ghoul. So, maybe he isn't physical now, not solid at all. So what is he then? His final speech makes use of Christian imagery – "We don't live alone. We are members of one body" – as well as prophetic warnings which remind us of the Old Testament, that a time will come when men who ignore his warning "will be taught it in fire and blood and anguish". As this language is also being used to enforce the author's socialist concerns, is the Inspector also, in a sense, Priestley himself? Is the Inspector Nemesis, the spirit of divine retribution in classical mythology punishing those who suffer from hubris? Is the Inspector the conscience of each of the Birlings, voicing the moral sense they have each submerged? Is the Inspector God coming to us on the Day of Judgment when all things shall be brought to light? He is all these things. The Inspector has become elusive, insubstantial. He is no longer "solid" at all. He is spirit, reminding the Birlings and the audience that not everything in this world is solid, material, and ripe for conquest and possession.

FIVE FACTS ABOUT J.B. PRIESTLEY AND *AN INSPECTOR CALLS*

1.

Priestley presented a weekly BBC radio broadcast called *Postscript* during the Second World War. It was enormously popular, with 16 million people – a third of all radio listeners – tuning in every Sunday.

2.

An Inspector Calls was first performed in Moscow in 1945 as no London theatre was available.

3.

Priestley declined a peerage in 1965. He did, however, accept an Order of Merit from the Queen in 1977.

4.

Basil Dean, the director chosen for the first London production, had such a short temper he was known to many in the industry as 'Bastard Basil'. He was sacked after the dress rehearsal.

5.

Priestley was regularly spied on by MI5 because of his left-wing sympathies. Previously secret files released in 2014 revealed the agency intercepted letters and calls for years after the war.

How does Priestley connect Eva and the Inspector?

Looking at Eva and the Inspector, we see how alike they are in being multiple, elusive. What is also interesting, is how they relate one to another. He is her spokesman, of course, but there's more to it than that. We have noticed how Eva refuses to "blame" Gerald, how she treats Eric as a "kid", how she internalises their treatment of her through her suicide. She completes their abuse towards her. Where is her anger? Where is her resentment? Where did they go? She seems to rise above these most natural, inevitable emotions. The answer is that she has repressed these feelings, and that her suicide (as we have seen) is also an expression of these unconscious, hidden feelings of anger towards the Birlings, and a demand for retribution – this is where the Inspector comes in.

Following this line of thought, the Inspector can also be interpreted as being a repressed part of herself, Eva's unconscious anger against those who have victimised her. He may be her unconscious feelings, or an alter ego, or even a ghost who is returning to demand retribution from those who have wounded her. (But wouldn't *she* be the ghost, in that case, haunting the Birlings? No, she can't be. She's not yet dead, so the Inspector is a kind of proxy for her.) He is psychological, he is supernatural. He is himself, but he is also enacting Eva's hidden feelings, her unfulfilled wish for revenge or justice. Each of them adds to the complexity of the other as a character.

Eva and the Inspector are alike in being elusive, difficult to grasp. There is a photograph of Eva, and a "rough sort of diary". These bring her back for a moment, but they also remind us she is gone. She is both a presence and an absence. Gerald adds to the sense of her elusiveness, when he asks *"but how do you know it's the same girl?"* Hoping to discredit the investigation, he asks if the Inspector may have shown photographs of different girls. The Birlings, indeed, *want* her to be lots of girls, because then they won't be guilty of harming her. They try to take her identity away from her all over again, but this fails, of course. The telephone rings, and they learn a "girl has just died" after all, and they're back on the hook.

In the play as a whole, then, Eva and the Inspector each grow in symbolic meaning and resonance. Whereas the Birlings and Gerald are presented in fairly straightforward terms, Eva and the Inspector also win another kind of victory as they become the most complex and compelling figures in the play. This is not an accident. Priestley is working here to grant them a symbolic and imaginative power over their opponents. The Inspector is more than a mere police inspector.

Eva represents much more than one girl. As the Inspector says, there are "millions and millions and millions of Eva Smiths". At the end of the play, they have a power over the audience as well as the Birlings. In this play, how Priestley presents his characters has a political effect and purpose.

What kind of play is *An Inspector Calls?*

An Inspector Calls can be difficult to pin down. It borrows from different kinds of drama, and the way these forms are combined is significant and effective.

As the curtain rises, we are presented with elements of realism. The audience is invited to look through "the fourth wall" into a dining room, with all its "substantial and heavily comfortable" furniture. Overlapping with this impulse towards the real, the play is naturalistic in the way it occurs continuously within a single space and time frame, the way it presents the Birlings as the products of their society and culture, and in the depiction of the "sordid" elements of Eva's life and death. It resembles Shaw's social realism, in its didactic purpose, its concern to correct social wrongs. Shaw wrote *Mrs Warren's Profession* (1893) to expose "the economics of prostitution" (J.L. Styan), while "*Widower's Houses*" (1892) was (in

Shaw's words) "deliberately intended to induce people to vote on the Progressive side at the next County Council election in London", regarding the issue of slum landlords.

As is often pointed out (by Benedict Nightingale, for example) *An Inspector Calls* is also a morality play. Thus, Eva is Everywoman, navigating the world, beset by personifications of vice and virtue. Within the allegorical pattern, we might have figures of Avarice (Birling), Anger or Envy (Sheila), Lust (Gerald), Pride (Mrs Birling) and Intemperance, Lust, and Sloth (Eric). Here, as in its social realism, the play becomes a vehicle of values, expressing Priestley's belief in charity, social connectedness and "community" over the values exemplified by the Birlings, whether these are viewed in allegorical or realistic terms.

In terms of dramatic form, the play begins in realism and moves into allegory, and even the supernatural, becoming a ghost story of sorts. We discover Eva was yet to die when the Inspector arrived to begin his questioning. Was he a ghost, a vengeful spirit demanding retribution? Is the play a kind of revenge tragedy, where a ghost makes the guilty pay for what they did? Is it an allegory of the Day of Judgement?

Why does Priestley move between these different dramatic forms in the play?

The naturalism establishes the *materialism* of the Birlings. It presents their "substantial furniture", their enjoyment of food and drink, and their dinner dress (compared with the poverty, hunger, and loneliness experienced by Eva). It also suggests the limitations of their world. This naturalism begins to trap them. The play occurs in one time frame, one space, and one continuous action. The lighting changes from "pink and intimate" to "brighter and harder". The characters are enclosed, under examination, unable to escape their "responsibility" for Eva's death. The naturalistic stage increasingly suggests their own limitations, and their inability to escape them.

This naturalism also makes what follows more credible. Imperceptibly, the play makes us *look again*, see allegorical meanings, that characters represent vices perhaps, or that the Inspector may be the conscience of the Birlings, or a figure representing God. Priestley uses naturalism to present the materialism of the Birlings – and he uses allegory and the supernatural to dismantle it. He gradually erases the world he creates. This is to show that "reality" is not what the Birlings think it is. "Reality" is not limited to that world of physical objects, conspicuous consumption, and economic values which the Birlings espouse. There are other kinds of value than these: social, moral, spiritual. Thus, Priestley makes a purposeful transition in dramatic form in the play. He does this to achieve a subtle dematerialisation of the world he presents, to reinforce the play's criticism of a materialistic way of looking at the world. His form is an aspect of his meaning.

What makes it a success on stage?

Drama thrives upon tension. There are two kinds in drama: conflict and suspense. *An Inspector Calls* has both in abundance. As we have seen, the Inspector's arrival generates rich conflicts between himself and the Birlings, and disputes within the Birling family. The more Birling, his wife, or Gerald resist the Inspector, the more opportunity there is on stage for opposition. The more the family divisions open up, between Sheila and Gerald, or between the Birling children and their parents, the more interest there is for us in the contests before us. And there are lots of them.

The detective story plot also creates suspense. When the investigation is under way, we are waiting to see how each character was implicated in Eva's death. This effect is heightened by the cliffhanging endings to Acts One and Two, as Gerald, and then Eric, await the Inspector's enquiries. In Act Three, moreover, there is the new interest raised by the new questions: was the Inspector real? Was it the same girl? Is a girl even dead? Finally, the news a girl has died sweeps the carpet from under the Birlings' feet, and provides us with the poetic justice we wish for, and new thought-provoking questions about the whole play.

The play's structure also works well. Structure in art is about the relationship between the various elements. It is about patterns. There can only be three kinds of patterns in a play or any art object. Things can be similar: repetition. Things can be different: contrast. Things can change: development.

An Inspector Calls makes very effective use of such patterning. The murder mystery plot uses repetition. The Inspector insists on following "one line of inquiry at a time". In Act One he won't show Gerald or Eric the photograph of Eva which has just upset Sheila. They have to wait their turn. Eric wants to "turn in", but the Inspector warns him not to do so, as he may need "to turn out again soon". Each character has to wait his or her "turn". This builds tension, as we wait to see how each person affected Eva. This also reinforces the dominant dramatic presence of the Inspector. He is in control. Lastly, this methodical sequence shows all characters are *equal* in the Inspector's eyes. When the Inspector insists upon taking turns, he is insisting upon fairness and justice. These values are the very ones which have been missing from the way the Birlings have treated Eva. The Inspector is restoring them. The very structure of the play here reflects Priestley's concern with social justice.

Contrast also adds to meaning and effectiveness. As the play opens the Birlings are "celebrating a special occasion, and are pleased with themselves". The family are coming together to celebrate the engagement – but the play ends with a very different mood. The engagement has been broken, because of Gerald's infidelity. Eric has been exposed as a drinker, a sexual aggressor, a thief. Lies have come to the surface. Family harmony has gone. Passing the port has given way to passing the blame. Eric, so quiet at the start, now violently berates his father and mother. Harmony is replaced by mutual recrimination. This contrast exposes the reality beneath the surface of the Birling family, and answers the questions which hovered above the opening scene. This, Priestley is saying, is where self-interest leads.

The contrast between the Birlings "before" and "after" is effective in unmasking their hypocrisy, and showing again how they cannot escape their responsibilities to be truthful and loving to each other if they wish for harmony. The contrast shows their sins coming home.

The dramatic structure also highlights development. How different Sheila is now from the submissive daughter of the start, apologising for interrupting: "I'm sorry, Daddy. Actually I was listening." The play has been painful for her. She "runs out" of the room when she recognises the photograph of Eva – but she returns, and accepts what she has done. She is incisive when she realises Gerald has betrayed her. She grows in self-awareness. Self-awareness had once been a matter of admiring herself in a pretty dress in a mirror at Milwards. No longer. She unsparingly examines her own guilt. She takes the Inspector's lesson to heart, and will not unlearn it. The structure of the play reflects Priestley's concern that we learn "responsibility", and contrasts Sheila's development, with the responses of her parents, and Gerald's response.

The play also has an inner dynamic, which makes the ending satisfying. The injustices Eva has experienced upset our equilibrium. The cruelty towards her arouses our anger, our sense of fair play. The plot engages us, and creates a demand for retribution, or justice. At the end, Priestley heightens our anxiety about this. We fear the Birlings and Gerald will get away with it. They don't. Our indignation and anger is carefully aroused – and discharged as the trap finally closes around the Birlings, with the final ring of the telephone.

When we heat it ring – "sharply", according to the stage direction – we remember "the sharp ring of the front door bell" at the beginning when the Inspector first arrived, interrupting Birling's thoughts about "community and all that nonsense".

So why does the bell ring?

In these moments, Priestley is surely remembering the famous and magnificent words of John Donne in *Meditation XVII* (1624), where the ringing of a funeral bell leads Donne to reflect how human lives are more interconnected than we think. In Donne's eyes, we share our mortal natures, and are required to recognise our duties to one another. In the most famous words of the *Meditation* we see a Christian reflection upon the theme of mutual responsibility which is at the heart of Priestley's play, and his political purpose in writing it:

> No man is an island, entire of itself; every man is a piece of the continent, a part of the main. If a clod be washed away by the sea, Europe is the less, as well as if a promontory were, as well as if a manor of thy friend's or of thine own were. Any man's death diminishes me because I am involved in mankind; and therefore never send to know for whom the bell tolls; it tolls for thee.

AN INSPECTOR CALLS: SOME CRITICAL VIEWS

An Inspector Calls was first performed in Britain at the Old Vic, on October 1st 1946. It met with very mixed reviews. In the *Daily Mail* the next day Lionel Hale wrote:

> *Who is the Inspector? ... Did the dead girl ever exist? The theatre hates indecision. Mr Priestley, not making his own mind up, does not persuade us.*

Such ambiguities in the play also irritated the *Observer* critic J.C. Trewin:

> *The play shoots its question marks as the porcupine its quills... Presently we ask if the author can be speaking in symbols. Can the Birlings stand for that complacent world of 1912, tottering blindly to its fall?... Is, then, this omniscient inspector Priestley's idea of the angel with the flaming sword? Who can tell? He comes in such a questionable shape. He may be an embodiment of Conscience or the representative of the Celestial Watch Committee... or simply (as he claims) an Inspector Goole? Have it your own way, says Mr Priestley.*

Hale and Trewin see it is a weakness of the play that Priestley raises these questions, leaving the audience uncertain how to interpret the world of the play and its characters. Trewin goes on, indeed, to suggest other weaknesses:

> *The play, not a long one, could have been stripped to half its length; though their offence is rank we feel that the Birlings are hardly worth this elaboration, this prolonged rattling of skeletons...*

This comment contains two implications: that the Birlings lack the psychological depth required to engage us fully, and that the plot of the play can seem "prolonged", a danger which follows from its (intentionally) repetitive structure ("one line of enquiry at a time," as the Inspector says).

To another early critic, Vincent Brome, the involvement of the entire Birling family in Eva's story is unrealistic:

> *It quickly becomes evident that Priestley has overloaded the family with such unrelenting complicity that verisimilitude is threatened and only the dramatic pace of the play speeds aside doubt as the family uneasily examines its history.*

All of these reservations have been echoed by later critics. Reviewing a BBC adaptation in September 2015, *The Daily Telegraph* critic Anita Singh said the play has "the subtlety of a sledgehammer". In Priestley's world, said Christopher Stephens in the *Daily Mail*, "every Briton with money is eagerly grinding the faces of the poor, and the poor are too busy being downtrodden to do anything about it". It is hard to deny that the play is didactic, or the moral simplicity of its essentially socialist message. Stephen Daldry, who directed a successful production, first staged in 1987, has called the play "a call to arms" – though people respond to it, he adds, because "[it's] not just saying, "let's go out and get a different government". It's 'let's go out and get a new moral perspective'."

Priestley doesn't shock his audiences in the manner of a truly radical playwright like Bertold Brecht, says Matthew Sweet in *The Independent*. There is a cosiness about his work which is reassuring.

> *An Inspector Calls wouldn't inspire anyone to, say, throw a brick through the dining room window of a rich industrialist. It pricks your conscience, but it also congratulates you for having one. In 1992, Daldry's production was read by many theatregoers as a critique of Tory disregard of the Eva Smiths of the late 20th century. But audience members who were Conservative voters could take comfort from the historicism of the piece. The play is set in 1912. The villains represent 19th century, not 20th century values. For audiences in 1946 as well as 1992, the play was an attack upon the injustices of the past, not the present; a protest against the supposed moral hypocrisy of their grandparents.*

In this sense, says Sweet, the play fits well into the tradition of plays and films written and produced between the 1930s and 1960s, scoring "easy points" off the generations who lived before World War One. These plays – and films like *Gaslight* and *Pink String* – looked back to the pre-World War One era with disgust, imagining the past as a "foreign country full of impregnated mill girls and granite-faced patriarchs":

> *It becomes clearer if you then read Priestley's 1967 essay 'Disturbing', and note his criticism of John Osborne's generation of playwrights for sending their punters home in a troubled frame of mind. It is Priestley's subtle flattery, I suspect, which has extended the play's appeal to audiences which take a dim view of socialism.*

Tim Martin has made much the same point in the *Telegraph*. Priestley is a subtler playwright than he is sometimes assumed to be – Martin quotes the psychologist Carl Jung who praised Priestley's mystical side, his "superhuman faculty of looking at things with a straight and an inverted eye". But the play, says Martin, comes packaged "with a kind of comforting period remoteness, and its presentation is that of a classic drawing-room thriller in the Agatha Christie mould"; its "creaky" detective plot works like a snake-charmer: because the surroundings are so unthreatening, the political aspect of the play is less obvious, and more palatable, than it might otherwise be.

THE PLAY IN ITS SOCIAL CONTEXTS

Priestley wrote *An Inspector Calls* in the winter of 1944, as he looked towards the end of the war, and the social changes he felt should follow. As Baxendale notes, Priestley was enormously influential in wartime Britain:

Broadcasting, journalism and public speaking made him a key wartime figure – perhaps, as Graham Greene would argue at the end of 1940, "a leader second in importance only to Mr Churchill".

Greene was thinking of moments like the broadcast following the retreat from Dunkirk (5th June 1940) where Priestley celebrated "how the little holiday steamers made an excursion into hell, and came back glorious". According to Greene, this broadcast "began to lead the way out of despair". In this broadcast, we can hear Priestley's concern with "the people", expressed in an avuncular voice and down-to-earth register which contrasts with (and complements) the magnificent oratory of Churchill.

For Priestley, indeed, 1940 offered an exhilarating glimpse of an England pulling together, overcoming class differences. He said "that in "that magnificent summer of 1940... I think I felt better than ever before or since. We lived at last in a community with a noble common purpose." For Priestley, the postwar settlement must reflect this communal effort by the people, as Baxendale again observes:

Priestley more than anyone became associated with the notion of the "People's war": that this was a war in which the active participation and commitment of ordinary people was paramount, and that this had implications for what the war meant, for the way it was run, and for what would happen after it was over.

He had been preparing for postwar reconstruction as early as 1941, when he wrote *Out of the People*, in essence a critique of the ruling class of the 1930s and of what Priestley saw as the entrenched interests which had prevented change after World War I. He was adamant there should be no repetition at the end of this conflict, and a new order should emerge to serve "the people, not a privileged few individuals but the people". Arguably, he was a highly significant figure in the evolution of the postwar settlement and the formation of the welfare state which followed Atlee's victory in 1945. Baxendale comments:

His reputation for political influence rests not only on his role in boosting wartime morale but on the perception that he contributed to a mood of popular radicalism which culminated in Labour's 1945 election landslide and the social-democratic era that followed.

In this context, it is easy to see how *An Inspector Calls* works to dramatise a need to embrace a vision of society based upon responsibility for others, the value of "community", and the interests of the many rather than the interests of the ruling few.

At the time when the play is set – 1912 – the ruling Liberal government had introduced reforms in old age pensions (1908) and introduced labour exchanges to help the unemployed find work (1909) and national insurance to provide people with free medical care, sick pay, and unemployment benefit (1911). It was the beginning of the welfare state, but then came World War One and Priestley felt that many of the gains which had been made were lost in the years which followed. He was determined to remind his audiences at the end of World War Two that one lost opportunity was enough. This time war must lead to reform, and a society which served the interests of the many.

Many feel the play's message is still relevant, one reason why it continues to be popular with directors and audiences alike. Indeed Ian McNeil, the designer of the 1992 production at the Lyttleton Theatre, said that his production team believed Inspector Goole's assertion that "[we] are members of one body. We are responsible for one another" could be read as a direct criticism of Margaret Thatcher's much quoted – and in McNeil's view "unacceptable" – comment that "there is no such thing as society" (a remark which, in the view of her defenders, is invariably quoted out of context: all she was trying to say, perhaps, is that people tend on the whole to rely on small communities rather than large ones). Left-wing commentators like Owen Jones and Andrew Sayer certainly believe that Priestley's sentiments are as relevant as ever today. In his book *Why We Can't Afford the Rich*, Sayer argues that "we are getting back to early 20th century levels of inequality between the rich and the rest". But even many conservatives believe inequality is still a major problem, among them the former prime minister, John Major, who has called for government, charities and the public to work together to deal with the problem.

In the world, if not in the play, there are two sides to the issues being raised – and another reading of *An*

Inspector Calls might challenge the 'socialist' argument at its core and deconstruct its ideological position. In a similar way, it is worth considering how Shakespeare might have handled the issues Priestley deals with, and how infinitely complex he would have made the debate between opposing voices in the play.

So, what would Priestley himself think, if he were still alive? We can only speculate – but he would surely be delighted by the way that his play is still being read, staged, and studied.

As a play, then, it has stood the test of time, the first and most important test of a work of literature. But just how good is it? John Baxendale thinks Priestley has a "problematical reputation within twentieth century culture". Although his work is by no means all pure realism, as we have seen, modernists like Virginia Woolf believed that he, like the novelists Arnold Bennett and John Galsworthy, was stuck in an Edwardian groove, his literary method, like theirs, ill-suited for dealing with what the modernists saw as the more fragmented reality of the modern consciousness. Art theorists like Clive Bell (married to Woolf's sister) argued that the formal qualities of an art work were the primary criterion of its worth. "Highbrow" art like Virginia Woolf's was moving away from the naivety of realism, and its social concerns.

Priestley, from this viewpoint, was an old-fashioned writer of "middlebrow" novels, essays, and plays. There was an element of class war involved in all this, of course: Priestley, the working class lad from Bradford taking on – and being taken on by – the pampered elite of the Bloomsbury set. Woolf, for example, wrote in her diary: "I invent this phrase for Bennett & Priestley 'the tradesmen of letters'", while Bennett and Priestley retaliated in kind with sarcasms about "the High Priestess of Bloomsbury".

Priestley was not an accomplished artist like Woolf, but he was a prolific and popular writer. He wrote *An Inspector Calls* in a week. As for whether it is art or not – well, that depends on what you believe art actually is, what it's for and who has the right to decide what is art and what is not. Some modern scholars, as John Baxendale notes, believe it is patronising to dismiss "middlebrow" writing, seeking to rescue it from what E.P. Thompson as called "the immense condescension of posterity". If *An Inspector Calls* is not great art, it is nevertheless a highly resilient play which is still relevant, rewarding and more subtle than its detractors allow.

BIBLIOGRAPHY

John Baxendale, *Priestley's England: J.B. Priestley and English Culture,* Manchester University Press, 2014

Vincent Brome, *J.B. Priestley,* Hamish Hamilton, 1988

John Donne, "Meditation XVII" (1624) from *Devotions upon Emergent Occasions, Together with Death's Duel,* Ann Arbor, 1957

John Elson, *Post-War British Theatre Criticism,* Routledge, 2015

Sigmund Freud, "Mourning and Melancholia" (1917) from *The Standard Edition of the Complete Psychological Works of Sigmund Freud,* Volume XIV, Vintage, 2001

Kim Greengrass, *An Inspector Calls : A resource pack for teachers,* The Magenta Partnership , 1999 (source of Ian MacNeil's comments on the National Theatre production of 1992)

Owen Jones, *The Establishment, and How they get away with it,* Penguin, 2014

Karl Marx and Frederick Engels, *Selected Works,* Lawrence and Wishart, 1968

Kerry-Anne Mendoza "Austerity: The demolition of the welfare state and the rise of the zombie economy", *New Internationalist*, 2015

Benedict Nightingale, *An Introduction to 50 Modern British Plays*, Pan, 1982

J.B. Priestley, *An Inspector Calls*, Heinemann, 1992

J.B. Priestley "J.B. Priestley pays homage to the small boats of Dunkirk", (first broadcast 5th June 1940) BBC Online Archive

Andrew Sayer, *Why we can't afford the rich*, Policy Press, 2015

George Bernard Shaw, *Mrs Warren's Profession*, Broadview Press 2005

George Bernard Shaw, *Widower's Houses*, Wildside Press, 2009

J.L. Styan, *Modern Drama in Theory and Practice*, Cambridge University Press, 2003

Margaret Thatcher "Women's Own", (31st October 1987)

Notes

Notes

First published in 2016 by
Connell Guides
Artist House
35 Little Russell Street
London WC1A 2HH

9 8 7 6 5 4 3 2 1

Picture credit:
p.9 © Moviestore/Rex/Shutterstock

A CIP catalogue record for this book is available from the British Library.
ISBN 978-1-911187-09-7

Design © Nathan Burton
Assistant Editor:
Paul Woodward

www.connellguides.com